Exploration of the California Coast

EXPLORATION AND DISCOVERY

EXPLORATION
AND DISCOVERY

Exploration of the California Coast

The adventures of Juan Rodríguez Cabrillo,
Francis Drake, Sebastián Vizcaíno, and other
explorers of North America's west coast.

Clarissa Aykroyd

Mason Crest Publishers
Philadelphia

Mason Crest Publishers
370 Reed Road
Broomall PA 19008

Mason Crest Publishers' world wide web address is
www.masoncrest.com

First printing

1 3 5 7 9 8 6 4 2

Library of Congress Cataloging-in-Publication Data
on file at the Library of Congress

ISBN 1-59084-043-7

EXPLORATION AND DISCOVERY

Contents

The Shores of California

IN THE FALL of 1542, three ships were sailing north along the coast of the modern-day state of California. They were small ships—the largest was no more than 100 feet long. Their names were *San Salvador*, *La Victoria*, and *San Miguel*.

The men on board these ships were Spaniards. The head of their expedition was Juan Rodríguez Cabrillo. He was a soldier and *navigator* who had already served Spain in Cuba, Mexico, and Guatemala. Cabrillo could not have known how important his expedition would be considered hundreds of years later. Previous expeditions had explored the long, narrow *peninsula* of Baja California, although the explorers were not sure whether Baja California was a peninsula or an island. But on this expedition, Cabrillo and his men were about to make the first landing by Europeans on the coast of Alta California, the modern-day state. The expedition followed many years of Spanish exploration and conquest in the Americas.

An account of the voyage says that the ships sailed into "a very good, closed port" on September 28, 1542. They named it San Miguel, after one of the ships in the fleet. This port would later be renamed San Diego.

When Cabrillo and his men went on shore, they met some of the native inhabitants. During their exploration of Baja California, their encounters with the natives had mostly been peaceful. This first meeting of the Spaniards and the natives in Alta California, however, did not go so well. Most of the natives fled, and only a few stayed to communicate with the explorers. That night, the explorers were fishing when some of the natives shot at them with arrows. Three men were wounded.

The Spaniards may have wondered why the natives were so hostile towards them. According to an account of the voyage, they had not mistreated any of the natives whom they met. A couple of days later, when they commu-

"Alta" and "Baja" mean "Upper" and "Lower" in Spanish. Baja California, now a Mexican state, is still called by that name.

nicated with some of the natives by using hand gestures, things must have become clearer. The account says: "Three large Indians came to the ships and explained that some people like us, that is, bearded, dressed, and armed like those on board the vessels, were going about inland . . . these were killing many of the native Indians, and for this reason they were afraid." The natives might have been referring to the inland expedition of Francisco Vásquez de Coronado, who had explored Arizona, Texas, and other areas of the American southwest a few years earlier.

While the Spanish ships were still in San Miguel, a storm passed over, "but nothing of it was felt, as the port is so good." After staying about five days in the port, Cabrillo and his men lifted anchor and continued north. As their journey progressed, the account says that they saw beautiful valleys and fine plains. "The country appears to be excellent," the account concluded. The expedition would end in disaster for Cabrillo, however, only a few months later.

Cabrillo's expedition was a turning point in the history of exploration of the west coast of North America. Before his expedition, no one had sailed as far north as Alta California. Cabrillo would be followed by other daring explorers, including a famous Englishman named Francis Drake. All of them hoped to win glory for their homeland and riches for themselves.

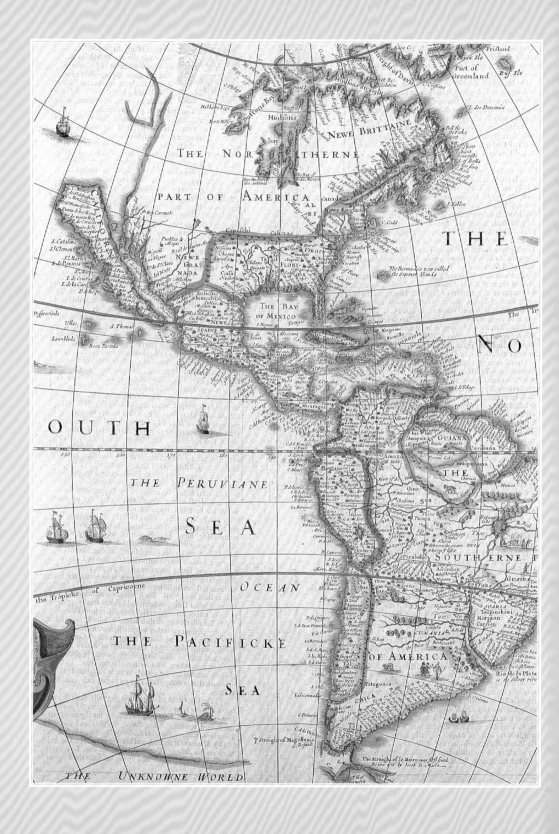

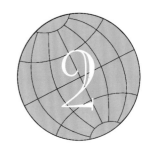

America and the Arrival of the Spanish

THE SPANISH SPENT 50 years exploring the Americas before they reached Alta California. By that time, they had already conquered the West Indies, Mexico, and many parts of Central and South America. Their arrival forever changed the lives of the native inhabitants of these places.

Before the arrival of the Europeans, there were more than 100 native tribes in California. They spoke different languages and *dialects*. Often, one tribe would not be able to understand another tribe at all, even if the distance between them was not very great. The tribes were linked by trade, and serious fighting between tribes was not very common. Their lifestyle depended partly on whether they lived

Shamans among the native peoples of California included rain doctors, who claimed to control the weather; rattlesnake doctors, who prevented or cured snakebite; and bear doctors, who were believed to change themselves into grizzly bears so as to attack enemies.

in a mountainous area, near the sea, or on another type of land. However, most of them were hunters and gatherers. Their most important foods included the acorn, different kinds of berries, and fish, where it was available.

When the Europeans began their conquest of California, they thought that its native inhabitants were *primitive*. In fact, the natives created beautiful works of art as part of their culture, including baskets with complicated designs. Some tribes made rock paintings. Their religion was so important to them that it could not really be separated from any other aspect of their lives. Each tribe had different religious practices, but they all believed in the importance of respecting nature, since they saw gods and spirits in everything around them. Their religious leaders were *shamans*, powerful men who practiced magic. When the Spanish arrived, they converted the natives to Christianity and introduced a completely new culture to them. They often did this by means of violence and enslavement.

California was inhabited by several Native American tribes when the Spanish arrived there in the mid-16th century. The top photograph shows a kicha, or living shelter, as built by the Juaneno Indians of California. At the right is a basket made of loosely woven willow leaves by a Kumeyaaay tribe member on the Campo Indian Reservation.

Hernán Cortés

Hernán Cortés was born in Spain to noble parents. As a boy, he served as an assistant in one of the churches of his town, Medellín. He went to Salamanca for his education. His parents wanted him to take up a career in law, but Cortés chose not to do this. Instead, he became a soldier and went to the West Indies in 1504.

Cortés spent a few years on the island of Hispaniola, now called Santo Domingo. In 1511 he joined Diego Velásquez in his conquest of Cuba. He became an important official in the town of Santiago.

In 1518, Velásquez put Cortés in charge of an expedition to Mexico. The expedition was supposed to claim the mainland for Spain and establish a colony. The conquest of Mexico took Cortés only a few years. He started a settlement in Mexico, which he called New Spain.

In 1524, Cortés went on an expedition to Honduras. This proved to be a mistake. The officials who ruled New Spain in his place did such a bad job that Cortés lost favor with Spain. Eventually, a viceroy was chosen to rule in place of Cortés.

After his Pacific expeditions, he went back to Spain in 1540. He died in 1547 near Seville.

Why were the Spanish the first to arrive in California? In the late 15th century, Spain was eager to conquer new lands, convert the inhabitants, and find new sources of riches. The goal of Spain and other European countries was to find a sea route to the Indies, or Asia. Sailing east was not practical because of the gigantic landmass of Africa. In 1492, an Italian *mariner* named Christopher Columbus sailed across the Atlantic Ocean. His *patrons* were the king and queen of Spain. His *provisions* included a letter of introduction to the emperor of China. No one realized that there was another continent in between. When Columbus landed on the islands off the east coast of America, he believed that he had reached the Indies.

Because Christopher Columbus had claimed the lands he discovered for Spain, that country was given the right to conquer and colonize the New World. The fact that the Americas were already inhabited did not bother the Europeans. The motto of the Spanish explorers was "God, gold, and glory." They wanted to convert the natives to their religion, Christianity, find gold to enrich themselves and their country, and win glory and fame as conquistadors.

Montezuma, the ruler of the Aztec empire, may have believed that Cortés was a god named Quetzalcoatl, or the Feathered Serpent. Cortés arrived in Tenochtitlán in 1519, a year that the Aztec calendar associated with Quetzalcoatl.

Columbus made a few more voyages to the Americas. By 1498, he had come to the conclusion that this was "a very great continent, until today unknown." From this time on, the Spanish set out to rule over a great empire in the Americas. They had competition from Portugal and France. Spain, however, used the islands of the West Indies as a base for trade and for their conquest of America. A major step toward the eventual exploration and colonization of California was Hernán Cortés's conquest of Mexico.

Cortés began the conquest in 1519, when he sailed from Cuba. He brought with him a large army and 16 horses. Cortés's expedition was officially under the direction of Diego Velásquez, the governor of Cuba. But soon after landing in Mexico, Cortés made a complete break with Velásquez. He and his soldiers marched through the Mexican jungle, all the way to Tenochtitlán, the capital of the native Aztec empire. Through a combination of force and political cunning, Cortés conquered Tenochtitlán and the Aztec empire by the late summer of 1521. Mexico now belonged to Spain. Tenochtitlán, which was eventually renamed Mexico City, became the capital of a Spanish government that ruled over Spain's territories. An account written by Bernal Díaz del Castillo, one of Cortés's soldiers, asked this question about Cortés's expedition: "What men have there been in the world who have shown such daring?"

Spain continued to expand its American territories after Cortés's accomplishment. Cortés was interested in exploring north along the Pacific coast. The exploration of Baja California began in the early 1530s. One of the first Europeans to arrive in Baja California was none other than Cortés himself.

A cliff juts into the Sea of Cortés in Baja California. The waterway between mainland Mexico and the Baja peninsula received its name from the Spanish conquistador who ordered it to be explored. During the early years of the 16th century, most Europeans believed Baja California was a large island.

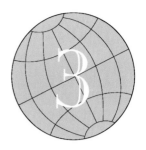

The Exploration of Baja California

THE EARLY SPANISH explorers were obsessed with the idea of undiscovered islands. Maps of the Americas from the late 15th and early 16th centuries show many islands that actually did not exist on both the east and west coasts of the Americas. Rumors about legendary islands came from imaginative stories written by Spanish authors of the time. The explorers believed that if they could find these islands, they would also find people with strange customs, beautiful women, and great riches. It was easy for them to think that Baja California was an island, because it seemed to be surrounded by water on all sides. They did not know that in the north it was attached to the American continent.

Cortés had ships built along the western coast of Mexico so that he could begin to search for his Pacific islands. In 1532, he sent out the first expedition to California by sea from the Mexican port of Acapulco. The expedition, however, was disrupted by one of Cortés's rivals, Nuño de Guzmán. The ships eventually sailed north and disappeared. Another expedition, sent out in 1533, ended in a mutiny on one of the ships. The mutineers sailed up the Gulf of California and landed on an island. This "island" may actually have been an island, or it may have been Baja California. Whatever the case, natives killed most of the mutineers when they tried to land.

At this point, Cortés decided that it was time for him to personally take command of an expedition to the mysterious island. In 1535, he set sail with three ships from the Mexican port of Chiametla for Baja California. On May 3, he landed at La Paz, which he called Santa Cruz. This first attempt at colonization was not suc-

Francisco de Bolaños may have been the first to give California its modern-day name. For a long time, the name only applied to Baja California. It came from a popular Spanish romance, which talked about an island ruled by a legendary queen named Calafia. Some historians, on the other hand, think that Cortés may have given Baja California its name.

cessful. The ships sent back to bring provisions ran aground because of a storm, and Cortés's men suffered from hunger and sickness. Cortés abandoned the colony not long after and returned to Mexico.

However, this was not the end of Cortés's interest in California and the Gulf of California. In fact, he became even more fascinated with California after hearing reports of fabulous riches on the northwest coast of America. Francisco de Ulloa, one of Cortés's officers, was chosen to lead another expedition to explore the Gulf. Although the **viceroy** of Mexico, Antonio de Mendoza, opposed the expedition, Ulloa set sail with three ships from Acapulco in July 1539. He explored north along the Gulf of California, finally reaching the head of the Gulf and the start of the Colorado River. Ulloa called the Gulf the Vermilion Sea. This was because of its red color, either from the mud of the Colorado River or from the red plankton found in the Gulf. Today, the Gulf is also known as the Sea of Cortés.

Ulloa and his men then sailed south along the eastern coast of Baja California, came around the southernmost tip at Cabo San Lucas, and sailed north again along the west coast of the peninsula. The expedition ran into high winds, which slowed down their progress. On his last attempt northward, Ulloa got as far as Cabo del Engaño, or the Cape of Deceit. The name suggests that Ulloa was disappointed about something. He had nothing good to say about the land and resources of Baja California. Also, he was probably hoping to find a *strait* through to the Gulf of California, which would make Baja California into an island. Ulloa's discoveries showed instead that Baja California was a peninsula. The belief that it was an island, however, returned after some time and persisted until the start of the 18th century.

While Ulloa was still exploring the west coast of Baja California, another expedition went north by land from Mexico to search for the riches of the northwestern coast. It was led by Francisco Vásquez de Coronado. This expedition spent most of its time exploring the present-day states of

Antonio de Mendoza was the first viceroy, or colonial governor, of New Spain. His laws provided a foundation for three centuries of Spanish rule in Mexico and the American southwest. In 1539 Mendoza sent a land expedition commanded by Francisco Coronado to explore the region north of Mexico, and he sent a sea expedition under Juan Rodríguez Cabrillo to explore the coast of California in 1542.

Francisco Vásquez de Coronado

Francisco Vásquez de Coronado was born in Salamanca, Spain. He went to Mexico in 1535 and became the governor of one of the Mexican provinces. In 1539, a monk who had been sent north to explore by the viceroy of Mexico returned with tales of great riches in the "Seven Golden Cities of Cibola." The monk was greatly exaggerating the wealth of some villages in New Mexico. But the Spanish were very excited, and Coronado was put in charge of a land expedition to seek the Seven Cities.

Coronado and his men captured native villages, but they found no riches. One group of Coronado's men became the first Europeans to see the Grand Canyon. Another group came close to the modern-day state of California, possibly entering it. In the spring of 1541, Coronado left many of his men in Texas and took a group north to Kansas. A native who they had captured had told them that the riches they were looking for could be found there. Once again, they only found simple villages. The expedition returned to Mexico in 1542.

Coronado became a provincial governor again after the expedition. Although the government was not pleased with his conduct during the expedition and his treatment of some of the natives under his control, he was still a powerful person at the time of his death.

The interior of Baja California was unforgiving desert, called *despoblado* by the Spanish explorers of the 16th century.

New Mexico, Arizona, and Texas. Coronado even went as far as Kansas. At one point during the expedition, a group of Coronado's men led by Melchior Díaz went to the head of the Gulf of California to look for a sea expedition that was supposed to meet them there. The two expeditions missed each other, though the leader of the sea expedition, Hernando de Alarcón, left some kind of marker to show that they had been there—probably a cross with a message carved on it. After finding this marker, Díaz and his men may have crossed the Colorado River and explored to the west. If they went far enough, they may have been the first Europeans to reach the modern-day state of California.

In 1541, the viceroy of Mexico sent another expedition to explore Baja California under the direction of Francisco de Bolaños. The viceroy still hoped to find a strait between the Gulf and the Pacific. Bolaños did not get very far before meeting a storm, however, and turning back. The next important explorer of the west coast would be Juan Rodríguez Cabrillo.

Tourists gaze at the view beyond this 14-foot sandstone statue of Juan Rodríguez Cabrillo. The monument was built for the 1939 San Francisco World's Fair; it is now located at Cabrillo National Monument in San Diego. Actually, no one is sure exactly what Cabrillo looked like; no portrait of the sailor exists today.

Cabrillo's Voyage

CORTÉS'S POWER DECLINED after his attempts at Pacific exploration, and he went back to Spain. With Cortés out of the way, the viceroy of Mexico wanted to send out some major expeditions for his own benefit. The Spanish still hoped to find rich "golden cities" in the northwest, though they had seen no sign of them so far. They also thought that if an expedition followed the coastline to the north as far as possible, they would meet up with the coast of China. The viceroy chose Juan Rodríguez Cabrillo to lead this new expedition. Cabrillo had instructions to establish friendly relations with the natives by trading with them, and to build settlements if he found a good place to do so. He had explored in Central America, but he had never before been the captain of a sea expedition. He left from the Mexican port of Navidad in June 1542 with three ships and about 250 men. They included soldiers, sailors, merchants, slaves, and a priest.

The explorers sighted Baja California less than a week after their departure. They sailed west around the tip of the peninsula and then continued north along the coast. An account of the voyage written after it was over describes the land that they saw in the early days as "level, bare, and very dry" on the flatlands and "high and rugged" on the mountains. The first place that Cabrillo gave a name to was Puerto de la Madalena. In some cases, they renamed places even though previous explorers had already given them Spanish names. They saw no trees on the land until they reached Asunción Point. At the start of August, they reached Cedros Island, named for its cedar trees. At this point, they were more than halfway up the peninsula of Baja California. One thing seems to have surprised them, since it is often repeated in the account: "[They] saw not a single Indian" and "They found no Indians, although they did find some signs of them."

On August 12, 1542, they had their first sighting of natives at Puerto de Santa Clara. The natives fled when they saw the explorers. After this point, they started to see

Juan Rodríguez Cabrillo

Historians are not sure whether Juan Rodríguez Cabrillo was from Spain or Portugal. He may have worked as a boy in Spain for a merchant. He probably added Cabrillo to his name because Juan Rodríguez was such a common name.

When he was still young, Cabrillo joined the Spanish army that conquered Cuba. In 1520, he was part of an army sent to Mexico by the governor of Cuba. This army was supposed to discipline Hernán Cortés. Cortés had disobeyed the governor of Cuba's orders and started the conquest of Mexico in his own way. But Cabrillo joined Cortés, along with many other soldiers. Under Cortés, Cabrillo commanded a group of crossbowmen.

Following the conquest of Mexico, Cabrillo explored Central America. He became a rich and powerful citizen of Santiago in Guatemala. He went back to Spain to find a wife, and he and his wife returned to Guatemala. In 1542, the viceroy of Mexico and the governor of Guatemala asked him to explore the California coastline. He was the first to explore the modern-day state of California. His career as an explorer ended on the California coast less than a year later, when he died from injuries after a fall.

natives quite regularly, and gave gifts to some of them. When one group told the explorers by hand signs that there were other Spaniards inland, Cabrillo gave them a letter to

The natives who the explorers met were mostly of the Chumash tribe, part of the Hokan family of California tribes. The Chumash were wealthy because of the large amounts of fish in their area. Some of their villages of round houses had as many as 1,000 people.

take to these Spaniards. He probably hoped that the letter would get to Coronado and his men. The account describes the land in this part of Baja California as "of very good appearance" with "good valleys."

During the month of September, Cabrillo and his men encountered more natives. On one occasion, "about forty Indians...brought roast maguey and fish to eat." The maguey is a type of cactus. Several days later, when they were on shore, they saw some natives in canoes. They also saw some strange animals that "looked like the sheep of Peru." These animals may have been pronghorn antelope.

On September 28, the explorers made their first landing in Alta California at the port that is now called San Diego. It was at this time that they had their first major conflict with some natives in which a few men were wounded. Still, the explorers and the natives seem to have left each other on a reasonably friendly note. The expedition continued north, discovering places like the islands of Santa Catalina and San Clemente, and Santa Monica Bay. Cabrillo and his men gave gifts to the natives and heard more reports of other Spaniards inland. They learned the names of some of the native villages, including Anacoac, Nocos, and Garomisopona.

Unfortunately, it was now a bad time of year to be a sea-going explorer. There were frequent storms, which were dangerous and prevented them from advancing as much as they wanted to. The sailors also suffered from sickness and hunger. The ships spent some time in the Santa Barbara Channel between a group of islands and the mainland. The channel protected them from the worst of the weather. When they left the channel in mid-October, the full force of a storm hit them, and they had to turn around. At the start of November, they stayed for several days in a place called Pueblos de Sardinas. The name came from the fact that they had stopped in this place earlier and the natives had given them sardines to eat.

In mid-November of 1542, the ships were separated for a few days by a heavy storm. The

Cabrillo named the mountainous area around Monterey Bay the Sierra Nevadas, or Snowy Mountains, because there was so much snow when he saw the coastline. Today, such snowy conditions no longer exist in the area because weather patterns are warmer.

main ship "turned towards land in search of their consort, praying God to *succor* her, as they very much feared that she would be lost." After regrouping, they sailed south to a bay that they had missed earlier in the storm. Today, the bay is called Monterey. They described the land in this part of California as snowy and mountainous. The sailors repaired their battered ships, then they sailed south to find a more sheltered place to spend the winter and anchored around the islands of San Miguel and Santa Catalina. In late December, some men went on shore to get water and some of the natives attacked them. Cabrillo rowed ashore to help. When he jumped out of the boat, he landed badly, breaking either his leg or his arm—possibly both. The wound became infected. On January 3, 1543, Cabrillo died. He was buried on an island that Cabrillo's men called Capitana, after their captain. This island was probably San Miguel, though no one is sure.

Bartolomé Ferrer, the first mate, was now in charge of the expedition. Before his death, Cabrillo had "charged him . . . not to fail to discover as much as possible of all that coast." The explorers tried to gather provisions and sail north again. They managed to sail farther north than they had with Cabrillo, perhaps as far as Oregon. But they did not have enough food, and they encountered a lot of bad weather. They spent a lot of time over the next few months seeking refuge from storms. At one point, one of the ships passed over some dangerous reefs. The account says: "The sailors made a vow to go to their church stark naked, and Our Lady saved them!" We do not know if the sailors actually did this after their return. Their vow may only have meant that they would go to church without any fine clothes or jewelry.

On April 14, 1543, the ships returned to Navidad. They did not get a warm reception. The viceroy was angry that they had not discovered a route to the Indies and that they had lost their captain and several other men. He was pleased that Cabrillo had made accurate records of the coastline in some places, at least. Guatemala honored him with a state funeral. Some of his sailors still felt that if Cabrillo had lived, he would eventually have reached the riches of the East. The Spanish government must have been unhappy to hear that there were no fabulous riches on the northwest coast of America and that much of the land was uninviting. Viewing Cabrillo's expedition as a failure, the Spanish showed little interest in California for close to 50 years. There is no evidence of any major exploration of California by the Spanish until the 1580s. They concentrated instead on their other possessions in the Americas, such as Mexico.

The English sailor Francis Drake was Spain's most feared enemy in the late 16th century. Drake led raids on Spanish ships and ports in the New World, and seized incredible treasure hoards. He found time to land in California and briefly explore the coast in the summer of 1579.

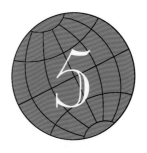

Drake's "Nova Albion"

UP UNTIL THE EARLY 19th century, the history of Europeans in California was almost completely dominated by the Spanish. However, there was one exception to this rule: the arrival of Sir Francis Drake in California. Drake was one of the most famous Englishmen of the age. His invasion of Spain's territory was part of an ongoing conflict between England and Spain.

For hundreds of years, France had been England's traditional enemy and main rival in Europe. However, by the 1570s, Spain was the dominant power in mainland Europe, and England's most dangerous rival. Spain wanted England to stay out of the Spanish territories in the Americas and

Sir Francis Drake

Sir Francis Drake grew up on a farm in the west country of England. His parents were tenants on a rich man's estate. The young Francis Drake became an apprentice on a small trading ship. He learned all about handling a ship and about using a compass and the stars to navigate. In his early twenties, he made voyages to the West Indies with trading ships owned by the Hawkins family. In 1572, Drake raided the Spanish territories in Central America, including Nombre de Dios in Panama. He crossed the narrow strip of land and saw the Pacific Ocean for the first time.

In 1577, Drake started his famous journey around the world. He reached the coast of Brazil in April 1578. Drake and his men met many natives along the coast of South America. Some were friendly, while others attacked and killed some of Drake's men. After passing through the Strait of Magellan near the bottom of South America, Drake sailed north along the west coast of the continent. Events led to his landing in California. His journey around the world ended back in England in September 1580.

Drake eventually became mayor of Plymouth. He also continued to raid the Spanish territories in the Americas. Between 1586 and 1588, Drake was mainly responsible for stopping the Spanish armada from attacking England. He died of a fever while raiding Panama in 1596.

King Philip II of Spain (left) was the ruler of the most powerful empire in the world during the 16th century. England, ruled by Queen Elizabeth I, was a small, relatively weak island country. Yet England's fortunes were rising as Spain's were declining, thanks in part to the activities of Francis Drake and other bold English sailors. By the end of the century, England, not Spain, would be the world power.

allow Spain to have complete control over trade in these areas. England refused to do so. The situation was made much worse by the San Juan de Ulúa incident in 1568. Drake was on a voyage to the West Indies with John Hawkins, a famous English seaman. Their ships were caught in a storm, and they had to seek a safe port to perform repairs and get more water. They landed in San Juan de Ulúa, near Veracruz on the east coast of Mexico. Angry that the English had been infringing on their territory, a Spanish fleet attacked the English ships. Most of the English did not escape, though Drake and Hawkins both got away safely. After this incident, Drake became a bitter enemy of the

Drake was a member of a small English fleet that was attacked by the Spanish at the harbor in San Juan de Ulúa, Mexico, in 1568. He believed the attack was treacherous, and harbored a lifelong anger toward Spain.

Spanish. He devoted much of his life to acts of *piracy* against them. This, rather than an organized expedition, would lead to Drake's landing in California.

Drake's voyage around the world may have been partly to gain riches for himself by attacking the Spanish and partly to look for a good place to found an English colony on the west coast of America. In September 1578, he sailed for the first time into the Pacific Ocean. Some of the original six ships in the fleet had been sent home or abandoned. Drake executed one of the ship's captains, Thomas Doughty, for *mutiny*. The last ships were separated from Drake's ship, the *Golden Hind*, by a heavy storm in the Pacific. By November 1578, the only remaining ship was the *Golden Hind*.

Drake sailed north, attacking Spanish ports and ships. In December, he raided the Chilean port of Valparaíso, stealing gold and silver. He robbed at least a dozen ships in the harbor of Callao, Peru. In February 1579, he attacked a ship named *Nuestra Señora de la Concepción*, which was sailing for Panama. The ship

Drake had the reputation of being a gentleman, even among the Spanish. He loved music and books, and one of his enemies described him grudgingly as "not very cruel." When he robbed the ship *Nuestra Señora de la Concepción*, he gave gifts like tools, weapons, and clothing to the Spanish before letting them go!

was carrying so much gold and other valuable objects that the English spent three days moving the cargo from the Spanish ship to their ship.

Drake captured a few more ports and ships, but by now the Spanish were angry and they were looking out for Drake. Also, the *Golden Hind* was leaking because it was so full of **booty**. Drake had to find a safe way to get home. He kept sailing north, perhaps hoping to find the Northwest Passage around the top of North America. He probably came close to the modern-day Canadian border. He may even have reached the coast of British Columbia in Canada. Drake almost certainly went farther north in the Pacific than any other European had done before. In June, the *Golden Hind* had to turn around because of bad weather. Drake sailed south, still looking for a safe harbor to repair the ship.

On June 17, 1579, Drake landed in a harbor on the California coast. No one is certain where the harbor was, though it is thought to be somewhere in the area of San Francisco. It may have been Drake's Bay, Bolinas Bay, or San Francisco Bay. Drake called the area Nova Albion, meaning "New England." He said that he chose to name it after his own country because its white cliffs reminded him of Dover, on the coast of England. Drake's Bay fits this description most closely.

This painting shows Drake's ship, the *Golden Hind*, sailing through the Pacific. During his historic voyage from 1577 to 1580, Drake visited the coast of California before continuing around the world.

Drake and his men spent about five weeks on the California coast. They did not like the weather, complaining of "nipping colds," "thicke mists and most stinking fogges." They built a fort in case of attacks by hostile natives. In fact, all the encounters between the natives and the English invaders turned out to be peaceful. A large number of armed warriors arrived at the camp, but Drake gave them gifts, and they returned to their villages without attacking. On another occasion, the natives performed a ceremony during which they put a crown on Drake's head and a *scepter* in his hands. Drake took this to mean that they wanted him to become their king. These natives were of the Coast Miwok tribe. Drake and his men observed that they were fond of singing and dancing.

Accounts of Drake's voyage say that when he left California, he nailed a brass plate to a post to commemorate his visit and to claim the place for the Queen of England. A brass plate with Drake's name on it was found in the right area in 1936. However, because of the plate's chemical content and some peculiarities in the language and writing, most experts think that the plate is a fake.

When they realized that the natives were unlikely to do them any harm, the Englishmen decided to explore further inland. They found what they called "a goodly country." It was full of wildlife, including gophers and large herds of deer, and the soil was good. They visited more native villages and observed their customs. The Englishmen even used some medicines and lotions they had with them to try and relieve the pain of some natives who were ill. It was a more peaceful meeting between Europeans and American natives than any encounters between the Spanish and the natives.

On July 23, the *Golden Hind* lifted anchor and sailed away. The natives showed great sadness at their departure and lit fires on the hilltops to see them off. Drake sailed west across the Pacific, making stops along the way in the islands of the West Indies. He arrived back in England on September 26, 1580.

Drake's California landing was only a minor incident in his voyage around the world, which was one of the greatest journeys at this time in world history. He never returned, however, and no Englishmen came to the west coast of America for hundreds of years. The English later claimed Oregon on the basis of Drake's coastal exploration. Soon after Drake's visit, the Spanish began to show interest in California once again.

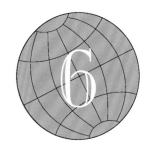

A modern-day recreation of a Spanish galleon plows through the water. Pirates often raided the galleons that carried treasure to Spanish ports in the New World, and from there back to Spain. This caused Spanish leaders to search for a place to build a safe port on the California coast where the ships could be protected.

The Search for a Safe Port

DURING THE 16th century, the Spanish used Mexico as a base for trade with the Philippines. At first, several ships went back and forth during one year, carrying valuable cargo. But since these ships were a constant target for pirates, the Spanish started sending only one ship per year between the Philippines and Mexico. The yearly ship was called the "Manila *galleon*," since it went from Manila in the Philippines to Acapulco in Mexico. The Manila galleon tried to take the least-risky route. Unfortunately, pirates often managed to seize the ship, especially off Baja California. Even if they got there safely, the ship and its crew were often in bad shape by the time they reached

Mexico. The Spanish turned their attention once again to California, hoping to find a safe port where the Manila galleon could get supplies and repairs on the way to Mexico.

In the 1580s, a few captains of Manila galleons explored the coast of California on their way from the Philippines. One of them was Francisco de Gali in 1584, who gave a good report on what he saw of California. Another was Pedro de Unamuno in 1587. He left the Philippines in July and arrived off the California coast in October. The ship anchored in a bay which Unamuno named Puerto de San Lucas, probably modern-day Morro Bay. Unamuno obviously thought that this port might be just the sort of place he was looking for. In his account of his explorations, he said: "In this port there is an unlimited quantity of fish of different kinds, trees suitable for masts, water, firewood, and abundant shellfish with all of which a ship in need could supply itself."

However, Unamuno did not meet with much success when he and his men tried to make contact with the native inhabitants. When he went on shore with a group of soldiers and a priest, the natives fled. A couple of days later, he led another group inland "as secretly as possible." They found some abandoned villages, but no people. Eventually, Unamuno decided "that it would not be wise to advance farther into unknown territory with so few men, without supplies, and that it would be best to return towards the ship." When they did so, a group of natives attacked them and the ship, killing one man and wounding several others. The Spaniards fought back and killed several natives. Although they later gave gifts to some of the natives, the situation again fell apart into fighting. Unamuno decided that it would not be a good idea to attempt any more inland exploration. Heavy fog prevented them from viewing the coastline properly. They sailed home as quickly as possible, disappointed by how badly the expedition had turned out.

Just after Unamuno and his men returned to Mexico, the Englishman Thomas Cavendish captured a galleon called the *Santa Ana* off Baja California. This was a blow to the economy of Mexico and the Philippines, because the ship had been filled with treasure that was being sent back to Spain. One person who suffered a financial loss from the galleon's capture was Sebastián Vizcaíno, a wealthy merchant. The success of pirates like Cavendish off Baja California led to more rumors that there was a strait somewhere on the peninsula between the Gulf of California and the Pacific Ocean where the pirates could lurk. The viceroy of Mexico wanted to turn California into a safe, colonized area so that explorers could search for the strait more easily. Also, they badly needed a port where ships could stop on their way back to Mexico.

In 1595, a Portuguese associate of Vizcaíno's named Sebastián Rodríguez Cermeño was chosen to look for a good harbor on the California coast. As the commander of a Manila galleon, the *San Agustín*, he began his exploration on his journey from the Philippines. On November 6, a storm forced the ship to anchor in Drake's Bay, which Cermeño renamed San Francisco Bay. The Spaniards stayed there for about a month. They gave gifts to the natives and observed their customs carefully. On November 30, a storm drove the ship against the shore, destroying it. About a dozen people died, including a priest. In desperation, Cermeño ordered the crew to gather as much food as possible in the area as well as boards and other objects from the shipwreck that the natives had not already carried away. This started some fights between the Spaniards and the natives. In December 1595, Cermeño and his men set off in the *launch* of the *San Agustín*. A launch is a small boat used for going on shore. It was not meant for a long sea voyage.

On the journey from Manila to Acapulco, the Manila galleons carried silks, spices, perfumes, gems, and other items from China and India. On the return journey from Acapulco to Manila, the galleons' main cargo was silver. They also brought churchmen carrying messages from the Spanish government to the Spaniards in the Philippines.

Storms battered the launch, and the men suffered badly from hunger. On one occasion, they became ill from eating some poisonous roots. Amazingly, they made it back to Mexico in January 1596 with no deaths reported. Cermeño had even managed to make charts of much of the coastline along the way. The Spanish government was still displeased, however, mainly because of the loss of the galleon. Also, they were still not sure where to find a good stopping place for the Manila galleons.

The adventures of Sebastián Vizcaíno in the early 17th century provided Spain with accurate maps of California and a better idea of what the country was like. Eventually, the Spanish would establish a system of missions throughout California. Many of the mission buildings can still be seen today.

Vizcaíno and Beyond

WHILE CERMEÑO WAS exploring California, Sebastián Vizcaíno had been making his own preparations. He mainly wanted to develop the pearl-fishing industry off California, but the government also wanted him to explore the area and maybe establish a colony. After many legal problems, including the threat of imprisonment, Vizcaíno set out from Acapulco in June 1596. He took three ships with him for his preliminary explorations. During a stop at Mazatlán, about 50 men deserted for no apparent reason. Vizcaíno kept going, however, and arrived at Baja California in early September. The bay where he landed on the east coast of the peninsula had been named Santa Cruz by Cortés. Vizcaíno renamed it La Paz. They were greeted by friendly natives, who even kneeled before a cross when they saw the Spaniards doing so. Vizcaíno felt that this might be a good place to build a settlement.

Vizcaíno explored further north up the Gulf of California, where he met with many problems. He threatened one group of colonists with death because they were unhappy with the quality of the land and wanted to go back to Mexico. A few days' sailing north of La Paz, Vizcaíno and his men ran into trouble when one of the Spaniards struck a native. Before this, the natives had been friendly, but now they attacked. As the explorers were trying to get back to the ship, their launch capsized, and 19 men drowned. A few days later, a fire destroyed much of the La Paz settlement. Vizcaíno returned to Mexico in December 1596.

Vizcaíno petitioned the Spanish government for support to return to the Gulf of California. But after a few years had gone by, the government was more interested in mapping the western coast of California. They wanted someone to chart the coast as far north as Cape Mendocino, near the northern border of modern-day California. Because of his experience, the government put Vizcaíno in charge of the expedition. They ordered him on penalty of death to ignore the Gulf of California on this voyage.

Vizcaíno left Acapulco with three ships on May 5, 1602.

Sebastián Vizcaíno

Not much is known about Sebastián Vizcaíno's early life. He was born in Spain and trained to be a soldier. In the 1580s, he came to the New World. After a few years, he became a merchant in the Philippines, where the Spanish had an important trade center.

Vizcaíno suffered a financial blow when the English pirate Thomas Cavendish captured a Manila galleon off Baja California in 1587. He decided to form a company that would harvest natural resources from Navidad, Mexico to California. They were especially interested in pearls. The company got permission for this undertaking in 1593. They were also supposed to explore the coast of California. Vizcaíno's first expedition to Baja California was in 1596.

Vizcaíno's main expedition took place in 1602. He got as far north as Monterey. After his exploration of California, he once again became involved with the Manila galleons. He also spent some time in Japan. In 1615, he defended the Mexican port of Salagua against the Dutch. As a reward, he was made alcalde, or mayor, of Acapulco.

About 200 men went with him. After being delayed by winds for some time, the expedition sailed west around the southernmost tip of Baja California and continued north

Some Spanish officials believed that instead of using Monterey as a port for the Manila galleons, they would do better to use the Islas Rica de Oro and Rica de Plata, an island group supposedly located somewhere off Japan. They thought that by the time the galleons reached Monterey, they were already too close to home for the port to be really useful. Spanish explorers, including Vizcaíno, were still searching for these islands as late as 1612, but they never found them.

along the coast. The ships were separated more than once. They sailed north for a few months, making detailed charts of the coastline. Their encounters with natives were mostly friendly. In November, they reached the bay that Cabrillo had named San Miguel. Although Vizcaíno was not supposed to rename the places he came to, since others had already discovered and named them, he usually did so anyway. He renamed this bay San Diego, after one of the ships. It still bears this name today. According to an account of the voyage, they met a native woman on the land who was "over 150 years old."

North of San Diego, Vizcaíno charted and renamed islands, including Santa Catalina and Santa Barbara. In mid-December, they arrived at the same port where Cabrillo and his men had repaired their ships after a storm in November 1542. Vizcaíno named it Monterey, after the viceroy of Mexico. He praised its sheltered location and its supply of natural resources, calling it "the best port that could be desired." Others who saw the bay later on were disappointed because it was not quite as wonderful as Vizcaíno had suggested. He was sure that it would be a good stopping place for Manila galleons and an ideal location for a colony.

Vizcaíno's men were suffering badly from **scurvy** because of a lack of fruit and vegetables. Two of the ships returned to Acapulco with few survivors. Vizcaíno's ship, the *San Diego*, went as far north as Cape Mendocino before turning around. During a storm, Vizcaíno fractured his ribs. Even worse, most of his men were ill from scurvy. It was important that they get home as quickly as possible. During a stop at the Mazatlán Islands, the men ate fruit. This improved their health somewhat. The *San Diego* arrived in Acapulco on March 21, 1603.

Vizcaíno did not make many new discoveries. Still, his expedition was important in two ways: he made excellent maps of the California coast, including placenames that are still in use today, and he convinced the Spanish government that they should colonize Monterey. However, not long after Vizcaíno's return, a new viceroy of Mexico was appointed. The new viceroy did not want to follow the accomplishments of his forerunners. He decided to ignore

Vizcaíno's suggestions. After 1606, the Spanish government officially discouraged the exploration of California.

Over the next 50 years, the Spanish became more interested in converting the natives in their territories to Christianity. The leaders in these efforts were the Jesuits. They were members of the Society of Jesus, a part of the Catholic Church. The Jesuits wanted to convert other nations to Christianity. Some of them also accomplished a lot in the way of exploration. Starting in the 1590s, they established *missions*, or religious settlements, in northwestern Mexico. In 1697, the Jesuits got permission to build missions in Baja California. Juan María Salvatierra founded the first mission in Baja California at Loreto in the same year. The Jesuits built many more missions on the peninsula in the years that followed.

In 1767, the Spanish government expelled all Jesuits from its territories in America. At this time, many countries were expelling the Jesuits because they feared they were getting too powerful. Another religious group called the Franciscans replaced them and took over their missions. A Franciscan named Junípero Serra was put in charge of the 15 missions in Baja California. In 1769, he founded the first mission in modern-day California at San Diego.

After the founding of the missions, Spain's relations with California changed. Although there were further voy-

A statue of Father Junípero Serra stands in a mission courtyard. In 1769, Serra founded the first Spanish mission in what today is the state of California, at San Diego.

ages of exploration, Spain was no longer an uncertain intruder looking in on California from the outside. The establishment of the California missions allowed the Spaniards to finally achieve its goals: the conversion of the natives to Christianity, and the increase in riches and glory for Spain.

Chronology

1492 The Italian mariner Christopher Columbus leads an expedition for Spain to find a western route to the Indies (Asia); in October, the expedition reaches the islands of the West Indies. Columbus does not realize that he has discovered another continent.

1498 On a third voyage to America, Columbus and his men set foot on the American mainland for the first time in Venezuela.

1508 The Spanish begin to colonize Jamaica, Cuba, and Puerto Rico.

1519 Hernán Cortés sails from the West Indies to Mexico with an army to begin the conquest of the Aztec Empire.

1533 On an expedition sent out by Cortés, Fortún Jiménez lands on the southern tip of Baja California; Jiménez and many of his men are killed in a fight with natives.

1535 Cortés leads an expedition to Baja California; the Spanish colony at La Paz is a failure.

1539 Francisco de Ulloa begins to explore the Gulf of California and some of the western coast of Baja California.

1540 Francisco Vásquez de Coronado and his men explore the American Southwest; a side expedition led by Melchior Díaz ventures near or into the modern state of California.

Chronology

1542 Juan Rodríguez Cabrillo leads an expedition north along the coast of California; he becomes the first European to land on the coast of modern-day California.

1579 The English explorer Francis Drake lands somewhere on the west coast of America, possibly at Drake's Bay in California.

1587 Pedro de Unamuno explores Morro Bay, but meets with hostility from natives; soon after, the English privateer Thomas Cavendish captures a Manila galleon off Baja California.

1596 Sebastián Vizcaíno tries to establish a colony at La Paz.

1602 While exploring the California coast, Vizcaíno arrives at the Bay of Pines and renames it Monterey.

1697 The Jesuit priest Juan María Salvatierra founds the first mission in Baja California at Loreto.

1769 The Franciscan friar Junípero Serra founds the first mission in Alta California at San Diego.

Glossary

booty—prizes or riches taken in war.

dialect—a type of language particular to a specific region.

galleon—a heavy, square-rigged ship used for war or trade.

launch—a small boat carried on a larger ship.

mariner—a person who navigates or helps in navigating a ship.

mission—a group of buildings belonging to the people of a church who are assigned to spread the church's faith to others.

mutiny—a rebellion against legal authority, especially by soldiers or sailors refusing to obey orders and attacking their officers.

navigator—somebody who is experienced in the art of plotting a course and directing a ship or other vessel on that course.

patron—a wealthy supporter of a person or cause.

peninsula—a portion of land jutting out from a main body nearly surrounded by water.

piracy—an act of robbery on the high seas.

primitive—pertaining to an early stage of development.

provisions—a supply of needed materials, especially food.

scepter—a staff or baton held by a ruler as a symbol of authority.

Glossary

scurvy—a disease caused by lack of vitamin C, which was common on long sea voyages. Its signs include spongy gums and loose teeth, soreness in the arm and leg joints, and bleeding into the skin and mucous membranes.

shaman—a person who uses magic for the purpose of curing the sick and controlling events.

strait—a narrow body of water that joins two larger bodies of water.

succor—to provide help or relief to somebody or something.

viceroy—the governor of a country or province who rules as a representative of the king.

Further Reading

Gallagher, Jim. *Sir Francis Drake and the Foundation of a World Empire.*
Philadelphia: Chelsea House, 2001.

Kelsey, Harry. *Juan Rodríguez Cabrillo.* San Marino: Huntington Library, 1986.

Mathes, W. Michael. *Vizcaíno and Spanish Expansion in the Pacific Ocean.*
San Francisco: California Historical Society, 1968.

Rice, Richard B., William A. Bullough, and Richard J. Orsi. *The Elusive
Eden: A New History of California.* New York: McGraw-Hill, 1996.

Wilson, Mike. *The Conquest of Mexico.* Philadelphia: Mason Crest, 2003.

Internet Resources

Juan Rodríguez Cabrillo

http://www.nps.gov/cabr/juan.html

http://www.win.tue.nl/cs/fm/engels/discovery/cabrillo.html

http://lcweb.loc.gov/rr/hispanic/portam/cabrilho.html

Francis Drake

http://www.mariner.org/age/drake.html

http://www.mcn.org/2/oseeler/voy.htm

http://www.legends.dm.net/pirates/drake.html

http://www.nmm.ac.uk/education/fact_files/fact_drake.html

Sebastián Vizcaíno

http://www.sandiegohistory.org/bio/vizcaino/vizcaino.htm

http://www.donaldlaird.com/landmarks/counties/100-199/128.html

http://www.dsusd.k12.ca.us/educational/explorers/vizcaino.html

Index

Photo Credits

About the Author

Clarissa Aykroyd is a graduate of the University of Victoria, BC. Her articles and fiction have appeared in several journals (*The Heroic Age, Critique, Canadian Holmes*) and newspapers (*The Vancouver Sun, Victoria Times Colonist*). Her interests include history, Arthurian legend, Sherlock Holmes, and music.